To Market, To Market

WRITTEN BY Anne Miranda
ILLUSTRATED BY Janet Stevens

McGraw Hill SRA
Columbus, OH

SRAonline.com

SRA

Printed in the United States of America

Send all inquiries to:
SRA/McGraw-Hill
4400 Easton Commons
Columbus, OH 43219-6188

ISBN 978-0-07-612525-8
MHID 0-07-612525-4

11 12 13 14 15 MER 25 24 23

The McGraw-Hill Companies

To my grandmother, Hattie Evans,
who used to bounce me on her knee
—A. M.

To Coleen Salley, who allowed me to
take her to market, to market;
to Shirley Sternola, for her encouragement;
and, of course, to Dorothy
—J. S.

To market, to market,
to buy a fat **PIG**.

Home again, home again, jiggity jig!

To market, to market,
to buy a red **HEN**.

Home again...

Uh-oh!

That pig
left the pen.

To market, to market,
to buy a plump **GOOSE**.

Home again...

Uh-oh!

The hen's
on the loose.

To market, to market,
to buy a live
TROUT.

Home again…

Uh-oh!

The goose
was let out.

To market, to market,
to buy a spring
LAMB.

Home again…

Uh-oh! Away the trout swam.

To market, to market, for one milking **COW**.

Home again...

Uh-oh! Where is that lamb now?

To market, to market,
to buy a white
DUCK.

Now the cow disappeared,
and I'm out of luck!

To market, to market, for one stubborn

GOAT.

The duck
flew the coop.
and the goat
ate my coat!

THIS IS
THE
LAST
STRAW!

I'm a shopping
disgrace.

Everything's
running
all over the place!

The **PIG**'s
in the kitchen.

The **LAMB**'s on the bed.

The **COW**'s
on the couch.

There's a **DUCK** on my head!

The **HEN**'s in the cupboard.

The **GOOSE** is there, too.

The **GOAT**'s in the closet—it's chewing my shoe!

The **TROUT**'s in the bathtub.
This place is a zoo!

I'm hungry, I'm cranky—
now what will I do?

To market, to market,

to buy some **POTATOES,**
CELERY,
BEETS,

and some ripe red
TOMATOES,

some **PEA PODS** and **PEPPERS,**

and **GARLIC** and **SPICE**,

a round head of **CABBAGE**,

a sack of **BROWN RICE**.

Add **OKRA**

and **ONIONS**

and one **CARROT** bunch.

Home again, home again—

hot **SOUP**

for lunch!